A

DOMESTIC

COOKBOOK

CONTAINING

A CAREFUL SELECTION OF USEFUL RECEIPTS

FOR THE KITCHEN.

BY

MRS. MALINDA RUSSELL,

AN EXPERIENCED COOK.

PUBLISHED BY THE AUTHOR.

PRINTED BY E. G. WARD, AT THE "TRUE NORTHERNER" OFFICE. PAW PAW, MICH.

1866.

DOMESTIC

COOKBOOK

CONTAINING

A CAREFUL SELECTION OF USEFUL RECEIPTS

FOR THE KITCHEN.

BY

MRS. MALINDA RUSSELL,

AN EXPERIENCED COOK.

PUBLISHED BY THE AUTHOR.

PRINTED BY E. G. WARD, AT THE "TRUE NORTHERNER"
OFFICE. PAW PAW, MICH.

1866.

A SHORT HISTORY OF THE AUTHOR.

I was born in Washington County, and raised in Green County, in the eastern part of Tennessee. My mother, Malinda Russell, was a member of one of the first families set free by Mr. Noddle, of Virginia. I am the daughter of Karon, the youngest child of my grandmother. My mother being born after the emancipation of my grandmother, her children are by law free. My mother died when I was quite young. At the age of about nineteen, I set out for Liberia ; but being robbed by some member of the party with whom I was traveling, I was obliged to stop at Lynchburgh, Virginia, where I commenced cooking, and at times traveling with ladies as nurse ; and always received the praise of being faithful. The following is a certificate given me by Doct. More at the time I started for Liberia:

"We, the undersigned, have been acquainted with Malinda Russell, a free woman of color, for the last eight or ten years, and certify that she is a girl of fine disposition and business-doing habits Her moral deportment, of late, has been respectable and we have little doubt, should she reach Liberia, in Africa, to which place she is now bound, that she will make a valuable citizen."

About this time I married in Virginia. Anderson Vaughan, my husband, lived only four years. I have always been called by my maiden name since his death, I am still a widow, with one child, a son, who is crippled ; he has the use of but one hand. While in Virginia, I kept a wash-house, The following is my advertisement ;

"Malinda Vaughan, Fashionable Laundress, would respectfully inform the ladies and Gentlemen of Abingdon, that she is prepared to wash and iron every description of clothing in the neatest and most satisfactory manner. Every article washed by her, she guarantees shall pass unscathed through the severest ordeal of inspection, without the remotest danger of condemnation. She can conscientiously boast of a proficiency in her business, and all clothing committed to her charge shall be neatly executed and well taken care of. She hopes to receive, as she shall exert herself to deserve, a sufficiency of patronage to insure her a permanent location. Her charges shall correspond with the times. — ABINGDON, May 3."

I returned to Tennessee, and. after the death of my husband, kept a boarding-house on Chuckey Mountain, Cold Springs, for three years. My boarders and visitors were from almost every State in the Union, who came to the Springs for their health, After leaving the boardinghouse, I kept a pastry shop for about six years, and, by hard labor and economy, saved a considerable sum of money for the support of myself and son, which was taken from me on the 16th of January, 1864, by a guerrilla party, who threatened my life if I revealed who they were. Under those circumstances we were obliged to leave home, following a flag of truce out of the Southern borders, being attacked several times by the enemy.

Hearing that Michigan was the Garden of the West, I resolved to make that my home, at least for the present, until peace is restored, when I think of returning to Greenville, Tennessee, to try and recover at least a part of my property.

This is one reason why I publish my Cook Book, hoping to receive enough from the sale of it to enable me to return home. I know my book will sell well where I have cooked, and am sure those using my receipts will be well satisfied.

PAW PAW, MICH., May, 1866.

RULES AND REGULATIONS OF THE KITCHEN.

― ― ― ―

The Kitchen should always be Neat and Clean. The Tablet Pastry Boards, Pans, and everything pertaining to Cookery, should be well Cleansed.

― ― ― ―

I have made Cooking my employment for the last twenty years, in the first families of Tennessee, (my native place,) Virginia, North Carolina, and Kentucky. I know my Receipts to be good, as they always have given satisfaction. I have been advised to have my Receipts published, as they are valuable, and every family has use for them. Being compelled to leave the South on account of my Union principles, in the time of the Rebellion, and having been robbed of all my hard-earned wages which I had saved ; and as I am now advanced in years, with no other means of support than my own labor ; I have put out this book with the intention of benefiting the public as well as myself.

I learned my trade of FANNY STEWARD, a colored cook, of Virginia, and have since learned many new things in the art of Cooking.

I cook after the plan of the "VIRGINIA HOUSEWIFE."

MALINDA RUSSELL.

RECEIPTS.

SALT RISING BREAD

To a half pint warm water, a pinch of salt ; stir to a thick batter and keep warm until it rises. To one pint of this rising add three pints warm water, a little salt, and a small piece of lard. Knead the dough until smooth, make into rolls, keep warm until it rises ; bake quick, but do not scorch.

SOFT GINGER BREAD,

Two quarts flour, 3-4ths lb lard, 3-4ths lb sugar, three teaspoonfuls cinnamon, two of ginger, one of allspice, one pint sour milk, molasses to make a stiff batter, one teaspoonful soda dissolved in milk.

SOFT GINGER BREAD.

One quart molasses, one cup sugar, 1-4th lb lard, three eggs ; beat sugar and eggs well together ; one gill sour milk, one table- spoonful soda dissolved in warm water, two tablespoonfuls ginger, flour enough to make a soft dough. Knead well, roll, and bake in a quick oven, Cream Cake,

One and a half cup sugar, two cups sour cream, two cups flour, one or two eggs, one teaspoon soda ; flavor with lemon.

SALLY DOUGH CAKE,

Three cups sugar, one cup yeast, three cups sweet milk, three eggs; beat to a thin batter, set over night. When light, add one cup butter, flour to make a stiff batter. Keep warm until it rises the second time. Paper and grease the pan before rising the last time ; bake in a slow oven.

WHITE MOUNTAIN CAKE.

One cup white sugar, two eggs, one-half cup butter, one-half cup sweet milk, one-half teaspoonful soda, one teaspoonful cream tartar, two and one-half cups flour.

QUEEN'S PARTY CAKE.

One quart sour cream, six lbs sugar, six lbs butter, five lbs raisins, five lbs currants, one and one-half lbs figs, one ounce cloves, one ounce cinnamon, one and one-half nutmeg, extract of lemon or vanilla, whites of eighteen eggs, yolks of ten eggs, one teaspoonful soda, two teaspoonfuls cream tartar, flour to stir quite stiff.

PLAIN POUND CAKE.

One lb sugar, one lb flour, one nutmeg, 3-4ths lb butter, twelve eggs, half gill brandy. Paper and grease your pans well; bake in a moderate oven.

CORK CAKE.

Three cups sugar, one cup butter, one cup sour cream, five cups flour, five eggs, one teaspoon soda, one teaspoon cream tartar; flavor with lemon.

SPONGE CAKE.

One lb sugar, twelve eggs; take out one yolk; ten ounces flour; beat the yolks and sugar together well; beat the whites to a stiff froth; gradually mix together; flavor with lemon; bake with a gradual heat.

DOVER CAKE.

Two cups sugar, four eggs, one cup butter, one cup sour cream, three cups unsifted flour, one teaspoon cream tartar, one teaspoon soda; flavor to taste.

WASHINGTON CAKE.

Three cups sugar, six eggs, one cup butter, one cup sour milk, one teaspoon soda, three cups flour, one teaspoon cream tartar; flavor with lemon to your taste.

BREAD DOUGH CAKE.

One pint light bread dough, three eggs, two cups sugar, one cup butter, fill with fruit or carraway seeds; stir together well, put in cake pan, let it rise, bake moderately. This cake, if made with fruit and iced, will keep a long time.

GRATED BREAD CAKE.

Grate one quart stale bread, six eggs, one and a half cup butter, three cups sugar, one pint milk, two teaspoons cream tartar, one teaspoon soda, one grated nutmeg, three tablespoons flour; bake in a moderate oven.

CREAM CAKE.

One cup and a half sugar, two cups sour cream, one teaspoon soda, three cups flour, lightly measured; one grated nutmeg; bake in a moderate oven.

FRUIT CAKE.

One lb fleur, one lb sugar, 3-4ths lb butter, two lbs seeded rai- ins, two lbs currants, one lb citron, one and a half lb almonds, half ance mace, one gill rose water, one wine-glass brandy, ten eggs.

WEDDING CAKE.

Three lbs flour, three lbs butter, three lbs sugar, six lbs currants, six lbs raisins, one ounce nutmeg, one ounce cinnamon, one ounce cloves, half gill brandy, one gill rose water, thirty eggs.

RICH BLACK CAKE.

Two cups sugar, one and a half cup molasses, two cups butter, one cup sour cream, four cups unsifted flour, eight eggs, one and a half lb raisins, one lb citron, one lb currants, one tablespoon mace, he do. cloves, one do. cinnamon, one wine-glass brandy, one do. rose water, extract of lemon.

FRUIT CAKE.

Four eggs, one cup sugar, two cups molasses, one and a half cup butter, one cup new milk, one lb raisins, two cups currants, one teaspoon soda, three ounces cinnamon, nutmeg, citron, four cups flour.

COCOANUT SPONGE CAKE.

Quarter lb white sugar, whites of four eggs, beat the eggs to a eroth, one tablespoon flour, one grated cocoanut ; mix the ingredients, bake in small shape, in a slow oven.

ALLSPICE CAKE.

Three-fourths lb butter, one lb flour, eight eggs, half teacup sour cream ; beat the yelks, sugar and cream together ; one tablespoon cloves, one do. cinnamon, one do. mace, one do. allspice, one gill brandy, lemon extract, one gill rose water, one nutmeg, one small teaspoon soda, one do. cream tartar, mixed in the flour ; bake in a moderate oven.

MARBLE CAKE.

THE WHITE.—Half lb butter, whites of fourteen eggs 3-4ths lb flour, half gill brandy ; flavor with lemon.

THE DARK.—The yelks of eight eggs, two teacups sugar, one do. butter, one do. sour cream, four cups flour, half cup molasses, flavor with cinnamon, cloves, nutmeg, or mace ; two teaspoons cream tartar, one do. soda ; beat the yelks and sugar together until very light. Paper and butter the pan, first a layer of the white, then of the dark, alternately, finishing with the white.

ELIZABETH LEMON CAKE.

Two cups sugar, one cup butter, one cup milk, five cups floUr, six eggs, one tablespoon cream tartar, rind and juice of one lemon.

ELIZABETH CAKE.

Three coffee cups flour, one and a half do. sugar, 3-4ths do. milk, one tablespoon butter, three and a half nutmegs, juice and rind of one lemon, 1-4th lb currants, one tablespoon cream tartar and soda.

CREAM CAKE.

Six cups sugar, six do. sour cream, twelve eggs, three cups buttery two teaspoons cream tartar, two do. soda, twelve cups flour; grate two nutmegs to flavor.

STIR CAKE.

One cup butter, one do. sugar, two do. flour, one do. milk, two eggs, two even teaspoons cream tartar, one do. soda ; flavor.

ALMOND SPONGE CAKE.

Three-fourths lb sugar, half lb flour, ten eggs ; beat the sugar and yelks together until light ; beat the whites to a stiff froth ; one and a half lb chopped almonds rubbed in flour stirred in ; add the whites of eggs, one gill brandy, half gill rose water, extract lemon.

BRIDE'S CAKE.

One lb sugar, one lb butter, whites of twenty-four eggs beaten to a stiff froth, one lb flour ; cream the butter, then cream butter and Sugar together ; mix gradually ; one gill brandy ; flavor with peach or lemon ; bake with gradual heat.

GOLD CAKE.

One lb white sugar, one lb flour, 3-4ths lb butter, yelks of twenty eggs ; beat sugar and eggs until light ; beat half the yelks with the sugar until very light, the rest with the butter ; mix together gradually one gill brandy and half gill rose water ; mix in the flour one teaspoon cream tartar, half do. soda ; bake in a slow oven.

RAISIN CAKE.

One lb sugar, one lb sugar, 3-4ths lb butter, twelve eggs, two lbs raisins chopped ; beat the sugar and butter together, add the yelks well beaten with butter and sugar, mix with the flour one teaspoon soda and cream tartar, add the whites beaten to a stiff froth, one grated nutmeg, and one gill brandy; bake by a gradual heat.

CITRON CAKE.

One lb sugar, 3-4ths pound butter, one lb flour, whites of twenty eggs, one lb citron, sliced thin and rubbed in flour; beat butter and sugar until light; one teaspoon cream tartar and half teaspoon soda mixed in the flour, one gill brandy, one do. rose water; flavor with peach or vanilla.

ROSE CAKE.

Three-fourths lb sugar, half lb butter, 3-4ths lb flour, whites of fifteen eggs beaten to a froth; cream the sugar and butter together; add the flour and whites of eggs, half gill brandy, flavor with lemon; one tablespoon cochineal with a small piece of alum tied in a bag soaked in warm water one hour. Grease paper your pan, spread a layer of dough, dip your bag in a solution of warm soda water, then squeeze the bag over the dough; add another laying of dough and cochineal alternately; bake with moderate heat.

LOAF JELL CAKE.

One lb sugar, 3-4ths lb butter, one lb flour, ten eggs beaten separately, one gill sour cream or milk, one teaspoon cream tartar, one do. soda, one nutmeg; mix and bake in a loaf until well done. Slice the cake while warm, and spread with jell, laying the slices together and icing the loaf.

GINGER POUND CAKE.

One pint molasses, half lb sugar, half pint sour milk, one teaspoon cream tartar, two do. soda, 1-4th lb lard; melt the butter and lard with the molasses until lukewarm, stirring all the time; five cups flour; beat the sugar and yolks together until light; one tablespoon ginger; add the whites, beaten to a stiff froth; ice while warm.

SPONGE CAKE.

One lb sugar, half lb flour, ten eggs, juice and grated rind of a lemon.

SEED CAKES.

Four cups flour, one and a half do. cream or milk, one half cup butter, three eggs, one half cup carraway seeds, one teaspoon saleratus, one do. rose water; make into a stiff paste; cut out with a tumbler; bake thirty minutes.

ALMOND SPONGE CAKE.

Eight ounces almonds blanched and pounded, two ounces flour, half pound sugar, the yolks of seven eggs, and the whites of five eggs.

QUEEN CHARLOTTE'S CAKE.

One lb flour, one lb currants, one lb sugar, half lb butter, four eggs, one gill brandy, one gill wine, one gill cream, spice to taste ; buke in a, loaf.

LOAF CAKE.

Two lbs dried and sifted flour, one pint new milk, blood warm, 1-4th lb butter, 3-4 ths lb sugar, one pint home-brewed yeast, three eggs, one lb stoned raisins, one nutmeg, a glass of wine if you like. Rub the butter and sugar to a cream, add the flour and the other ingredients; let it rise over night; bake one hour and a half in a slow oven.

LEMON CAKE.

One cup butter, three do. powdered sugar, rubbed to a cream, yelks office eggs well beaten, one teaspoon soda in a cup of milk, juice and rind of one lemon ; add whites of eggs beaten to a stiff froth; sift in four cups flour, and bake.

JELLY CAKE.

One half cup butter, two cups sugar, one cup milk, two eggs, two teaspoons cream tartar, one do. soda; mix a little stiff, bake thin ; when cold, spread with jelly.

FLANNEL CAKE.

One quart sweet milk, stir to a thick batter with flour, two tablespoons yeast; let it rise over night ; in the morning break in three eggs, stir in two tablespoons lard.

MUSH CAKE.

Make a thin mush ; add two tablespoons melted lard, one pint sweet milk, three eggs ; mix a batter to the consistency of pancakes. Pour the hot mush into the Latter, stirring it well; and bake one griddle.

COFFEE CAKES.

Bake soft boiled rice ; add twice as much flour as rice, a handful Indian meal, and a little yeast ; mix over night, and bake in the morning.

INDIAN CAKE.

Two cups meal, one do. flour, one do. cream, one do. milk, one do. sugar, three eggs, one teaspoon soda, one do. salt.

FRIED RICE CAKES.

Rub into a quart bowl of soft boiled rice One cup milk and two eggs ; mix till smooth ; put out in small cakes with flour enough to form them, and fry.

INDIAN MEAL BATTER CAKES.

To one quart Indian meal add one tablespoon lard, and enough hot water to scald the meal ; stir it smooth ; add enough sour milk to make a batter ; break in two eggs ; put into a pint of flour two teaspoons of soda and two do. of cream tartar ; stir this in last, and bake on a griddle.

RICE BATTER CAKES.

One pint rice ; after being cooked, stir in the rice while hot, half pint Indian meal, three eggs, one pint sour milk, one pint flour ; melt a tablespoon of butter or lard, stir in the butter, add more milk if too thick, one and a half teaspoon soda ; bake on a griddle.

DROP GINGER CAKE.

One pint molasses, one cup sugar, one do. sour cream, three eggs, one cup melted butter, three teaspoons soda, one do. cream tartar ; heat the molasses and butter together ; beat the sugar and eggs together ; put the soda and cream tartar in the flour, make a stiff batter, almost a dough ; one tablespoon ginger ; dr p into a buttered dripping-pan ; bake moderately, without scorching.

BOILED ICEING.

Beat the whites of four eggs to a stiff froth ; boil one lb crushed sugar until it ropes and spins off in threads ; then turn the boiling sugar slowly over the eggs, stirring thoroughly and beating ; flavor with lemon, peach, or vanilla.

SUGAR DROP CAKE.

One lb sugar, six eggs, one cup butter, one do. sour cream, half lb stoned raisins, half lb citron, two teaspoons cream tartar, one do. soda; chop raisins and citron fine; half lb English currants, one lb flour ; rub the fruit in four ounces more flour, beat the eggs separately, stir the fruit in last ; two teaspoons cloves, two do. cinnamon, one grated nutmeg, two teaspoons mace. Butter sheets of paper, lay in a dripping-pan, and bake moderately, iceing while warm.

STRAWBERRY SHORT CAKE,

Make the cake the same as cream biscuit ; crush and strain the berries, stirring them thick with white sugar, bake in sheets; split the cake while hot, butter well and cover with berries, stack in a Steak dish, turn sweet cream over it, and eat while hot for tea.

COLD ICEING.

One lb pulverized sugar, break in the whites of five eggs on the sugar, beating with a silver spoon or wooden paddle ; pound a lemon and squeeze in the juice,

RASPBERRY TEA CAKE.

One cup white sugar, one pint sour cream, three tablespoons melted butter, three cups flour, one and a half teaspoon soda, two do. cream tartar, grated nutmeg, mix into a batter; pour over sheet paper into dripping-pan ; bake in a quick oven ; when done, cut into squares, crush the berries, and sweeten to your taste. Cover the cake with berries, and stack the same as Gell Cake.

WAFER CAKE,

Three-fourths lb sugar, 1-4th lb butter, eight eggs, half lb flour ; cream the butter ; beat the yelks, butter, and sugar together until light, beat the whites to a stiff froth, add all together, stir to a batter, drop into greased wafer irons, bake in a minute, take while hot, roll them up and ice them.

OLD MAIDS.

Whites of three eggs beaten to a stiff froth, one cup white sugar, half cup flour, flavor with lemon, stir to a batter, and fry in hot lard. When done, grate white sugar over them.

BOILED ICEING.

One lb white coffee sugar, boiled until it ropes ; beat the whites of three eggs to a stiff froth ; turn the hot sugar slowly over the egg, beating until it cools, then flavor with extract of lemon.

SHORT CAKE.

One half lb butter, one pint sweet milk, soda the size of a bean ; mould quickly, not very stiff, roll into sheets, bake in a brisk oven.

FRIED CAKES.

Two and a half cups sugar, one cup sour milk, three eggs, one cup butter, one teaspoon soda; roll; cut with fried cake cutter.

LEMON CAKE.

Cream one lb butter and one of sugar together; beat the yelks of twelve eggs and add to the butter and sugar ; beat the whites to a stiff froth, add one lb flour and the whites gradually, one teaspoon soda and cream tartar, in the flour grate the rind and juice of a lemon ; bake in moderately ; flavor with extract of lemon.

PLUM CAKE.

One lb sugar, one do. butter, eight eggs, one lb flour, three lbs stoned raisins, three do. currants and citron, one glass wine, one do. brandy, one half teacup molasses ; spice to taste.

PLUM CAKE.

Three lbs flour, three do. ra sins, three do. butter, three do. sugar, thirty eggs, four lbs currants, half ounce cloves, one nutmeg, half lb citron, one tablespoon ginger.

SOFT GINGER CAKE.

One lb flour, one do. butter, nine eggs, two quarts milk, a little yeast ; mix together warm.

SOFT GINGER CAKE.

One cup butter, one do. sour milk, three do. molasses, five do. flour, three eggs, two teaspoons soda, raisins or currants.

GINGER CAKE.

One pint molasses, one cup butter, one pint milk, one tablespoon ginger, three eggs ; add flour to make a proper thickness to bake in pans.

SPONGE CAKE.

Eight eggs, one lb sugar, half lb flour, a little salt.

POUND CAKE.

One lb sugar, one do. flour, 3-4ths do. butter, eight eggs.

SWEET TEA CAKE.

One quart milk, one coffee cup butter, one lb sugar, yeast to raise.

NAMELESS CAKE.

One teacup butter, one do. sugar, five eggs, one cup milk, two cups flour.

SODA CAKE.

Three teacups sugar, one do. butter, five do. flour, the whites of seven eggs, two teaspoons cream tartar, a scant one of soda, one cup sweet milk, the grated rind of a lemon ; add the cream tartar to the flour, soda to the milk.

DROP CAKE.

One pint flour, half lb butter, half lb sugar, half of a nutmeg, a handful of currants, two eggs, a large pinch of soda; bake ten or fifteen minutes.

CHEAP SPONGE CAKE.

One cup flour, two eggs, one cup sugar, large spoon sweet milk, half spoon soda, one spoon cream tartar, a little salt, grated rind uf one lemon, one teaspoon butter; bake fifteen minutes.

SPONGE CAL E;

Two cups sugar, two do. flour, six eggs, two teaspoons of cream tartar. Put in the flour one teaspoon soda dissolved in a little milk, and stirred in when going into the oven.

NEW YEAR'S CAKE.

Three and a half lbs flour, 3-4ths lb butter, 1-4th lb powdered sugar, seven eggs, half ounce ammonia, half pint milk.

SHREWSBERY CAKE.

One lb flour, one. do. butter, one do. sugar, the whites of sixteen eggs, spice to your taste.

ICEING.

One lb sugar, whites of three eggs, cold water enough to wet the sugar. Beat the eggs a little, put them in the sugar ; let it boil until it thickens, stirring it thoroughly all the time.

FRENCH LADY CAKE.

Three cups sugar, one do. butter, six eggs, one cup sweet milk, one teaspoon soda, two do. cream tartar, one wine-glass brandy, the juice of one lemon, four cups flour ; the soda dissolved in the milk, the cream tartar in the flour.

GRAHAM CAKES.

One quart buttermilk, three eggs, one pint cooked rice, a little salt, one tablespoon cream tartar, half tablespoon soda, flour to make a thin batter ; bake on a griddle.

[REMARKS. — As a great many ladies have wished to know how I have such good success in making my cakes so light, I will say, I first heat the oven hot enough for cooking, set in my cake, and open the door ; and for a common sized cake leave the door open for about fifteen minutes, and for a large one, about twenty minutes. When the cake begins to raise, close the door.]

MRS. ROE'S CREAM PIE.

One cup good sweet cream, the whites of three eggs beaten to a froth, one cup coffee sugar, the juice of one lemon. Bake with a rich under crust.

CONELL RISING.

Take half a teacupful of conell with a little salt, turn boiling water over it, stir it quite thin, keep it warm ; set it one morning to bake the next. The bread made the same as salt rising bread, using two or three table spoonfuls of the yeast.

MUFFINS.

Seven eggs well beaten, one quart sweet milk, three tablespoons melted lard, a lump of soda the size of a bean, flour to make a thin batter. Butter the muffin ring, and bake in a quick oven.

GINGER SPONGE.

Two cups molasses, one do. sugar, one do. butter, five eggs, two cups sour milk, two teaspoons soda, two do. cream tartar, two do. ginger, one do. cloves, one do. cinnamon, five cups flour.

CINNAMON COOKIES.

One cup sweet cream, two do. sugar, three eggs, half cup butter, two tablespoons ground cinnamon. Beat the eggs and sugar well ; melt the butter; stir it with the eggs and sugar till smooth; then add the cream, one teaspoon cream tartar, half teaspoon soda, flour to make a soft dough ; roil thin, and bake in a quick oven.

GINGER CRACKERS.

One pint molasses, one pint sugar, one teacup lard, one Cup butter, one teaspoon soda ; melt the molasses, lard and butter together, until lukewarm; the yelks of eight eggs ; beat the eggs and sugar together till light; one tablespoon ginger, one do. cinnamon, one do. cloves, one do. lemon, one nutmeg. Add the ingredients together, with flour enough to make a stiff dough ; knead Well, roll thin, and bake in a quick oven; cut with cake cutters.

COOKIES.

One lb white sugar, one pint cream, one ounce ammonia ; flour to roll.

COOKIES.

One cup sugar, one do. sour cream, one do butter, one teaspoon soda ; flour to roll out.

COOKIES.

Three teacups sugar, four eggs, one cup butter, one do, sour milk, half teaspoon soda ; flavor to taste ; soft dough; roll thin, and bake in a quick oven.

JUMBLES.

One lb sugar, half lb butter, seven eggs, one nutmeg, one teaspoon cream tartar, half teaspoon soda, flour to make a soft dough, half teacup sweet cream ; cream the butter ; beat the sugar and eggs together until quite light ; roll and cut them ; bake in a moderate oven.

JUMBLES.

One lb flour, 3-4ths lb sugar, one half lb butter, five eggs, mace, rose water, and carraway, to your taste.

GINGER SNAPS.

One Clip molasses, half cup sugar, half cup butter, half clip boiling water, teaspoon soda, two tablespoons ginger ; pour the boiling water over the butter, dissolve the soda in the water and butter, then stir it to a cream ; mix all together, with flour to make a stiff dough, roll thin, and bake in a quick oven.

WHITE SUGAR CRACKERS.

Half lb sugar, 1-4th lb butter, whites of ten eggs beaten to a stiff froth, half lb raisins seeded and chopped, half tablespoon lemon, one tablespoon rose water. Cream the butter, beat sugar and butter together until light ; add the ingredients together, flour to make a soft dough ; run it through the jumble moulds, sprinkle it over with white sugar, bake in a moderate oven, ice when cool.

FLOATING ISLAND.

One quart rich sweet cream, one lb loaf sugar, one pint Cognae brandy, one gill wine, six eggs broken into the cream ; churn in a whip churn to a stiff froth, spread with gell slices of pound cake, and lay it in the bottom of a float dish, and turn the float over it.

BOILED CUSTARD.

Beat with six eggs sufficient sugar to sweeten the custard, then boil half gallon new milk ; stir in slowly the eggs and sugar, stirring all the time ; flavor with cinnamon bark, boiling it in the milk.

WHIP TRIFLE.

Two quarts sweet cream, sugar to sweeten, one pint wine, one gill brandy, juice of one lemon, whites of six eggs ; flavor with extract of lemon ; churn well in a whip churn, cut small pieces of sponge cake, laying it in a float bowl ; the trifle to be turned over it after taking off the froth—putting the froth in wine glasses and Betting around the float bowl.

WINE GELL.

Two packages gelatine, one quart wine, one quart Water. Put into a kettle and simmer, pounding and squeezing in the juice of two lemons, break in six eggs, simmer all together 20 or 80 minutes; pour into a flannel bag and let it drip ; the first that drips turn back into the bag, letting it drip again. Pour into moulds, and set it away to gell.

GINGER PUDDING.

One and a half cups molasses, half cup sugar, three eggs, one cup sour milk, half cup butter, three cups flour lightly measured, one teaspoon soda, one do. ginger, one do. cloves, bake in quick oven.

CHARLOTTE RUSSE.

One pint milk, 3-4ths lb sugar, halt' box gelatine. Put these together, and set over a kettle of boiling water after the gelatine is dissolved ; beat four eggs and stir in ; leave over the fire until it looks clear, then let it cool. Beat to a stiff froth one pint cream, add vanilla to taste; stir all together well and set in a cool place, with ice or snow around it. When you add the eggs, stir thoroughly ; when cool, give it a hard beat. Put cake in a mould stuck together with white of egg, and put the liquid inside, or serve the cake and liquid separately.

APPLE JELL.

One peck pared and cored tart apples, two quarts water: boil and strain through a bag without pressing ; let it drip over night; one pint sugar to two pints juice ; boil quickly to a gell.

BLACKBERRY WINE.

To one gallon berries pour over them one quart boiling water, crush the berries and strain through a hair sieve ; add three pounds sugar to one gallon juice, turn into a stone pot and let it stand till through singing, skimming every morning; tie over the top a thin cloth, bottle and cork tight when through singing.

BLACKBERRY CORDIAL.

Boil a sufficient quantity of berries to make a gallon of juice ; boil in a stone pot, setting it in hot water ; strain through a bag ; add three lbs white sugar to a gallon of juice ; when cool, pour in one quart brandy ; bottle and cork tight.

STRAWBERRY CORDIAL.

Two and a half lbs sugar to one gallon juice ; put the berries in a stone pot, setting it in hot water, boil and strain through a bag, mix the sugar with the juice, simmer half an hour ; when cold, add a quart of peach brandy, bottle and cork.

QUINCE CORDIAL.

Pare and core one half bushel quinces, putting into a brass kettle with two quarts water, cook well, drain through a sieve, and then through a bag, adding two and a half lbs sugar to a gallon juice ; boil 15 or twenty minutes. When cold, add one quart brandy to one gallon juice, bottle and cork.

RICE MILK.

One pint boiled rice to one gallon milk, twelve eggs ; sweeten to your taste, and flavor with lemon.

CHOPPED APPLE PIE.

C hop your tart apples, break in six eggs, half lb sugar, half lb butter melted ; beat all together, flavor with nutmeg and cinnamon, adding one gill brandy and one gill wine. Paste the plate, laying pastry over the top, and bake.

BAKED INDIAN MEAL PUDDING.

Make a thin mush, beat six or eight eggs, stir in the mush half teacup butter, make a batter thick of Hour and sweet milk, putting in the eggs. Stir the mush in the batter until smooth, grate in a nutmeg, bake slowly in a pudding pan ; eat with rich sauce.

BAKED APPLE PUDDING.

Pare and core twelve apples, put them into a pudding dish, with one cup sugar and two of water ; put in cloves and cinnamon ; set them in a slow oven to bake; beat the yelks of six eggs with one cup sugar, one pint milk, two tablespoons flour, turn this over the apples, and cook until done ; beat the whites of six eggs lightly with a little white sugar, flavor with lemon ; turn this over the fruit just before taking from the oven ; to be eaten with rich cream.

SPICED CURRANTS.

Five lbs ripe currants, five lbs sugar, two tablespoons cinnamon, two do. cloves, one pint vinegar; boil two hours, or more, till quite thick.

CURRANT JELLY WITHOUT COOKING.

Equal parts, of juice and sugar. Stir it for three hours, and put it in glasses. It will be firm jelly within three days.

CHOW CHOW.

One peck green tomatoes, half-a-dozen peppers, one dozen onions, grated horse-radish ; chop and scald in salt and water, drain in a sieve, put into jars and pour spiced vinegar over it.

LEMON JELLY.

One and a half ounces isinglass, one and a half lbs sugar, four lemons, throe pints boiling water. Lay the isinglass in cold water half an hour, take it out and put it with the sugar and lemons sliced. Pour on the boiling water, stirring it all the time ; strain through a jelly bag. In warm weather, it will require more isinglass to stiffen well.

TO CLARIFY SUGAR FOR PRESERVING.

For each lb of sugar allow half a pint of water; for every three lbs, the white of one egg. Mix when cold, boil a few minutes and skim ; lot it stand ten minutes, skim again, and strain it.

RIPE TOMATO PICKLES.

Prick tomatoes full of holes, let them stand in salt and water two days ; then put them into fresh water one day, then seald them in vinegar. Peel and slice one dozen onions ; put into a jar a layer of onions, tomatoes, ginger, pepper, mustard and cloves, alternately, until the jar is filled.

TOMATO CATSUP.

To one gallon tomatoes add four tablespoons cloves, one do, mace, one do, cayenne, two do. allspice, eight tablespoons of white mustard seed, two whole peppers, one ounce garlic, one pint good vinegar, Boil away nearly half, strain, bottle and cork tight.

RASPBERRY JAM.

Allow one lb of sugar to one lb of fruit ; boil the fruit half an hour; strain one quarter of the fruit, and throw away the seeds ; add the sugar, and boil the whole ten minutes.

GOOSEBERRY JELL.

Put your berries into a stone pot, set it in a kettle of boiling water, covering it tight ; let it stand until they burst ; run through a sieve, and strain through a bag. Allow one lb and a quarter sugar to one pint of juice ; boil quick to a jell.

RIPE CHERRY PIE.

Remove the stems and stones ; cover the bottom of a long tin with the fruit, to which add a teacup of sugar and one of flour ; bake with an upper and under crust,

CRANBERRY JAM.

One quart raw cranberries, to one lb white sugar. Simmer the fruit one hour after adding the sugar, stirring all the time. Put into bottles or jars, corking tight, Ready for any season.

PEACH MARMALADE,

Take clingstone peaches, peel and separate from the pits, put them into a preserving bottle, with water enough to cook them done ; mash them fine, and stir them until smooth, To every lb of fruit add 3-4ths of a lb white sugar, which is best to make them clear. Stir three hours, cooking slowly. This will keep two or three years by keeping it in sealed jars.

SPICED CURRANTS.

Five lbs currants, four lbs sugar, one cup vinegar, tablespoon cloves ground, two tablespoons pulverized cinnamon.

Dried Ripe Mulberries.

Stem and scald the fruit. Take one gallon berries to one and a half lbs sugar, drain them from the syrup, lay them on a platter, boil down the syrup quite thick, and turn it over the fruit. Set it in an oven to dry, be careful not to scorch them. To be used the same as raisins for cakes or puddings. Put them into glass jars and seal tight.

GREEN TOMATO PRESERVES.

Five lbs green tomatoes sliced, half tablespoon alum powdered, one tablespoon salt, one gallon water ; let them stand in this water twelve hours ; turn this off and put on fresh water, and let it stand two hours. Take five lbs white sugar, and water enough to make the syrup; put in the syrup, let it scald twenty minutes ; lift it out on a platter to stand twelve hours. Let the syrup come to a boil, turn in the tomatoes and boil one hour, then skim out the fruit and let the syrup boil. Put the fruit into jars — a layer of fruit sprinkled over with pieces of orange peel, grains of cloves, and pieces of cinnamon, alternately, until the jar is filled. Pour it over the syrup hot, and seal tight.

PEACH CORDIAL.

Pare ripe cling penches enough to make a gallon of juice; boil mid strain them ; add three lbs sugar, and simmer half an hour; when cool, add one quart peach brandy ; bottle and cork.

RIPE CHERRY PIE,

Stem and stone the fruit. Paste a large pudding dish, take out the cherries from the juice, fill the dish and cover with paste; set in the oven to bake, boil the juice quite thick, sweeten to your taste. When cold, add one pint sweet cream to the syrup; take off the top crust and turn the syrup over the cherries, returning the crust.

RIPE PLUM PUDDING,

One pint sour milk, half lb butter made into a dough, half teaspoon soda; roll into a large sheet half a gallon stoned plums; scald and flour the sack, put the sheet of dough into the sack, turn in the fruit and pinch the dough together at the top, tie the sack tight and boil two hours. For the sauce, half lb butter, and one lb butter; cream butter and sugar together ; break in three eggs, beat it until light; make it into rolls, to be sliced and eaten with the pudding.

BOILED BATTER PUDDING.

Three pints sweet milk, eight eggs, one teaspoon soda, two do, salt ; put into a bag, and boil three hours. Sauce — Rub together butter and sugar, break in three eggs, and stir till light; one grated nutmeg.

CHRISTMAS PLAM PUDDING.

One lb seeded raisins. one do. currants, one do. flour, half do. bread crumbs, half do. suet, ten eggs, 1-4th lb citron, and one pint milk. It should be boiled at least three hours; eaten with sauce composed of sugar, butter and brandy, beaten very light.

COLD WATER BISCUIT.

To one pint cold water, a piece of lard the size of a teacup, one and a half teaspoon salt ; work it lightly in the pastry bowl, turn out on the dough board, and knead and pound until it blisters. Mould into biscuit, and bake in a hot oven.

TO MAKE LARD PASTRY.

Two quarts flour, one and a half lb lard ; divide the lard into four parts; rub one part into the flour with a knife, mix with cold water to a consistent dough, roll the dough into sheets, spreading the remainder of the lard over them, folding the sheets and rolling again; salt-spoon of salt. Nice and flaky.

PUFF PASTE.

One and a half lb flour, 3-4ths do. butter; rub a quarter of the butter, together with two teaspoons cream tartar and half teaspoon soda, into the flour ; spread the remainder of the butter over the sheets, fold and roll again thin, and bake in patties for tarts.

RICE, PUDDING BOILED.

Pick and scald one quart rice ; stone two lbs raisins; rub rice and raisins together until thoroughly mixed, put in a bag into boiling water, boil one hour. Make a sauce of one lb butter, one and a half do. sugar, three pints water, one pint brandy, nutmeg and lemon.

WHORTLEBERRY BOILED PUDDING.

Eight eggs, one quart sour milk, two tablespoons lard, flour to make a stiff batter, a little salt. Sprinkle them with dry flour, rub them well, mixing them with the batter : scald the bag, and sprinkle it with dry flour; turn it in, leaving room to rise. Boil with or without a ham ; cat with cream sauce or wine.

SWEET POTATO BAKED PUDDING.

Boil six or eight large sweet potatoes, peel them, strain through a colander, separate six eggs and one cup sugar, beat the yelks and sugar together until light, mix the potato and one cup butter while the potato is warm ; beat the whites to a stiff froth, and add them last ; flavor with nutmeg, a cup sweet cream three tablespoons flour.

SLICE APPLE PIE.

Paste a pudding dish ; first a layer of sliced apples, sugar to taste, cloves, nutmeg, cinnamon, and ginger, alternately, until filled ; add half pint water and one gill wine ; cover with rich pastry and bake until done. To be eaten with sauce.

SWEET POTATO SLICE PIE.

Made in the same manner as above, adding one gill brandy, one do. vinegar, half pint water, one grated lemon, rind and juice, sugar to taste; paste the dish, cover the top ; eat with sauce.

COOKIES.

Two cups sugar, two do. sour milk, one cup butter, one teaspoon soda, one do. cream tartar, flour to make soft dough, ground Carraway seeds; sprinkle top with white sugar, roll and cut.

APPLE CUSTARD.

Boil and strain one quart apples, one half lb sugar, l-4th lb butter, six eggs, one pint sweet cream, one gill brandy, one gill wine ; beat the sugar and yelks together until light, melt the butler, cream the butter and apples together; separate the eggs, beat the whites to a froth, put the whites in last, flavor with lemon ; line a dish with paste, and turn in the custard ; bake in hot oven.

IRISH POTATO CUSTARD.

Boil and strain through a sieve one dozen good sized potatoes ; rub through the sieve with the potato half lb butter, half lb sugar, eight eggs ; cream together the sugar, yelks, and potato ; stir in one pint sweet cream, one pint brandy, one gill rose water ; lemon to the taste, Paste the dish richly made, fill the dish, and bake in a slow oven.

PAP CUSTARD.

One quart sweet milk, boiled and thickened very thick with flour, nearly half lb butter ; melt the butter in the boiling milk ; twelve eggs, the whites beaten to a froth, yelks and sugar one lb, creamed ; flavor with nutmeg and lemon ; add the whites before flavoring. Paste and bake in plates.

CHEAP GINGER BREAD.

One cup sugar, half cup molasses, two tablespoons melted lard, two cups soul milk, two teaspoons ginger, two do. soda. Mix to a soft dough, roll and bake.

CURVIES' PLUM PUDDING.

Three eggs, eight Boston Crackers, one pint milk, l-4tll lb melted butter, one and a half cup sugar, one and a half lb stoned and chopped raisins, half teaspoon nutmeg, half teaspoon cloves, half teaspoon cinnamon. Bake or steam three or four hours.

SALLY LUN.

Three tablespoons yeast, two do. butter, two do. sugar, two eggs, flour to make thick as cake. Let it rise six hours ; bake quick.

FRENCH TEA BISCUIT.

Two lbs flour, two ounces butter, half pint sweet milk, one egg, half cup sugar, one cup yeast, half teaspoon soda.

LEMON PUFF.

Six eggs, one pint sweet milk, five tablespoons flour, a little salt ; bake in cups full twenty minutes. Sauce — Juice of one lemon, put in as much sugar as yon can beat the whites of three eggs, pour over the top ; eat while hot.

CRULLERS.

Two cups sugar, one cup butter, one do. sour milk, six eggs, one teaspoon soda, grated nutmeg, flour to mix a soft dough ; boil in lard.

MARY'S JUMBLES.

One lb flour, half lb butter, 3-4ths lb sugar, five eggs ; any spice you like.

APPLE FLOAT.

Boil twelve large apples, remove the skin and strain through a sieve, beat the whites of ten eggs to a stiff froth, sweeten to the taste, and beat with an egg whip one hour, flavor with lemon ; to be eaten with cream.

BOILED TRIFLE.

One half gallon boiled milk, eight eggs, leaving out the whites of six ; beat the remainder with one half lb sugar till light; turn the boiling milk over the eggs, stirring briskly, then turn back into the kettle, stirring all the while ; boil six or eight minutes, flavoring with cinnamon or lemon peel. Beat the whites of six eggs to a stiff froth, turning in a glass of gell, beating well ; lay in a glass dish three or four slices sponge cake, pour over the cake one half pint brandy. When the trifles cool, pour into the dish, float it With the eggs and gell.

BUTTER PASTRY.

One lb eight ounces flour to one lb butter ; cream and beat all the water out of the butter ; have it firm. Quarter the butter into four quarters, taking out four ounces of the flour ; take one quarter of the butter and mix with the large quantity of the flour, stirring with a knife, not using the hand ; roll the dough very lightly, sprinkling over the sheets the remaining flour and spreading them over with the butter, folding and rolling alternately. Lay away the dough on the slab, leave it one hour, cut in small pieces, roll thin, lay three sheets in a patty and bake. To be used for tarts.

CREAM CRACKERS,

Half pint water, one quart sour cream, half lb butter, half teaspoon soda, flour to mix a stiff dough, knead it well until it blisters, as you do biscuit ; to this quantity of dough lay on 3-4ths lb butter, roll thin, spreading the butter over it, sprinkling with flour, folding and rolling again.

TO MAKE HOP ROLLS.

One quart warm milk, melt in it a small piece of lard; beat the yelk of one egg in one spoonful of sugar, mix in flour to make a stiff batter, stir in three tablespoons of hop yeast, set away to rise till morning, work in flour to make a soft dough; if sour, add a little soda, make into rolls, rise, and bake in a quick oven.

MINCE PICS.

Five lbs beef, four lbs suet, five lbs raisins, five lbs sugar, one lb citron, eight crackers pounded fine, two lemons chopped fine, three pints cider, one quart molasses, one quart wine, one quart brandy, one gill rose water, one quince boiled and chopped, two tablespoons salt, eight teaspoons cloves, thirteen do. cinnamon, four do. mace; grate nutmeg on the top of the pie; add bits of sugar before baking. Mix molasses, crackers, cider and spice together, beat to almost a scald, then mix it with the remainder of the ingredients. Mix the sugar with the wine; If you like them richer, add fruits, sugar, and spice.

CRACKER PIE.

One Boston cracker, one cup water, juice and grated rind of a lemon, one cup sugar, piece of butter the size of a butternut. This makes one pie.

SUMMER MINCE PIE.

Four crackers, one and a half cup sugar, one cup molasses, one do. cider, one do. water, two-thirds do. butter, one cup chopped raisins, two eggs well beaten, and stirred in the last thing. Brandy and apice to taste.

MOLASSES CUSTARD.

One quart molasses, eight eggs, half lb butter ; beat the eggs, then beat eggs and molasses together until light ; add ginger, nutmeg, and cinnamon.

LEMON CUSTARD.

Yelks of twenty-four eggs, one lb butter, two grated lemons ; grate peeling and press out the juice ; beat the butter, eggs, and one lb sugar together until very light, flavor with lemon acid, line the dish with paste, and bake.

GREEN CORN BREAD.

Three dozen ears of corn grated, one egg, milk, a little salt.

SODA ROLLS.

To one gallon flour add one full tablespoon soda, and sufficient sour milk to make a soft dough ; knead well, make it into large rolls. Grease your hands well with lard, pat the rolls rough, lay them into pans, and bake in a slow oven.

CREAM TARTAR ROLLS.

Three pints flour, a piece of butter half the size of a hen's egg rubbed into the flour ; mix through the flour one tablespoon cream tartar, dissolve in sweet milk one teaspoon soda, knead and pound well, make in small rolls, and bake in a quick oven.

INDIAN MEAL BATTER BREAD.

One quart Indian meal, half pint flour, three eggs, two tablespoons melted lard, one cup and a half of sour milk, half cup hot water, one teaspoon soda ; stir well together, bake in a quick oven.

TOMATO CATSUP.

One gallon tomatoes, four tablespoons salt, four do. cloves, one do. Cayenne, two do. allspice, eight. do. white mustard seed, two whole peppers, one ounce garlic, one pint good vinegar. Boil away nearly half, strain and bottle ; cork tight.

PICKLED STURTIONS.

Soak them three days in salt and water, then pour off the brino and pour on scalding hot vinegar.

PICKLED CAULIFLOWER.

Cook the cauliflower tender, put it in a jar, pour vinegar and good ground mustard scalded together over them.

PICKLED PEACHES.

To one gallon vinegar add four lbs sugar; boil and scum. Take clingstone peaches, fully ripe, rub off the down, stick into each three or four cloves, put into a stone jar, pour over them the boiling liquid, cover the jar closely, set in a cool place for a week or * two. Pour off the liquor and boil as before, then return it to the fruit boiling hot ; cover carefully for future use.

BRANDY PEACHES.

Three dozen largo ripe peaches, drop into hot ley, remove them quickly, rub off the fur, drop them into cold water, let them soak while preparing the syrup. Take three lbs sugar to one quart peach brandy, boil to a syrup, drop in the peaches, let them barely scald, lift them out on a platter and let them drip, put them into a glass jar, cook the syrup well ; before putting the syrup on, turn over them half a pint of peach brandy, then pour on the syrup, and put up in jars. Use white sugar.

PRESERVED PEACHES.

Five lbs sugar to five lbs peaches ; while the syrup is making prepare your fruit. Make the syrup of half the sugar, put tho peaches in the boiling syrup, cook about ten minutes ; dip them out and lay on platters until the next day ; drain off the juice from them, putting it with the remainder of the sugar into the kettle and boiling to a thick syrup before adding the fruit, which must cook a few minutes, then lift them out carefully and put in jars ; boil the syrup until waxy, then turn over the peaches.

PRESERVED QUINCE.

Prepare your syrup ; when boiling, pare and core your quinces, drop them in the liquid, and let them remain three or four minutes. Skim them out and lay on platters, then boil the syrup till thick ; drain the quinces, then weigh them, allowing one lb sugar to one lb of fruit ; put all in the kettle and boil about twenty minutes ; put the fruit in jars, and turn over them the syrup.

FRIED RUSK.

Two cups sugar, half cup butter, half cup yeast, half pint sweet milk, three eggs, flour to make a thick batter ; set away to rise ; when light mix to a dough, rise again ; roll ; cut and fry.

MUFFINS.

One pint milk, half cup butter, yeast and a little salt, flour to make a batter.

PICKLED PLUMS.

To seven lbs plums take three lbs sugar, one quart vinegar, spice to your taste. Scald every day until the plums are cooked.

JUMBLES.

One cup of sugar, one cup of butter, one egg, a lump of soda the size of a nutmeg.

CRACKERS.

One pint of milk, four ounces of butter, four eggs, flour as stiff as you can make it.

BURST-UP BICE.

Pick and wash a teacup of rice ; turn over it boiling water ; turn it off, and turn it into a pint of boiling water ; boil hard in a tin basin closely covered; cook dry; season when done. Bice cooked in this way is always white and nice.

ONION CUSTARD.

Pare and boil twelve large onions ; mash when cooked soft, and strain through a s'eve ; stir in, while hot, 1-4th of a lb of butter ; beat half a lb sugar with the yelks of six eggs; stir into the sugar three tablespoons flour, one pint rich cream ; stir all together until smooth

; one tablespoon cinnamon, half spoon cloves ; stir well ; beat the whites of the eggs, and stir it in last ; paste your pans with rich pastry ; bake in a quick oven.

CRANBERRY BAKED PUDDING.

Paste your pans with a thick rich crust, and cover it with berries ; add a little sugar if you like ; then cover with a thin crust, and fill with berries until four layings, then bake in a moderate oven ; eat with cream and sugar, or wine sauce.

BAKED BATTER PUDDING.

Twelve eggs, half gallon sweet milk ; beat the eggs until light ; flour to make a good'batter ; stir in a small teacupful of grains of allspice, a little salt to your taste. Bake in a deep pan or Dutch oven. To be eaten with sweet cream flavored with lemon or vanilla.

BUSK.

One lb sugar, seven eggs, half lb butter, one teacup good hop yeast, made into a stiff batter over night ; when light, work it into a soft dough in the morning ; let it rise again ; make it out into rolls; rise again; put a little soda in the flour if sour ; bake in a slow oven.

FRIED DOUGHNUTS.

One pint sour milk, three eggs, two tablespoons lard, one tca- . spoon soda, salt, flour to make a not very stiff dough. Roll into sheets, cut, and fry in boiling fat.

BAKERS' GINGER BREAD.

One quart molasses, quarter lb lard, three eggs, one gill sour cream, one tablespoon soda, two tablespoons ginger, half tablespoon cloves, one tablespoon cream tartar, flour to make a soft dough ; put the soda and cream tartar in the flour, knead well, roll, cut in squares, and bake on sheets.

PRESERVED ORANGES.

Boil the oranges till you can run a straw through the skin. Clarify 3-4ths of a lb of sugar for each lb of fruit. Take the oranges from the water, and pour the hot syrup on them. Let them stand one night ; next day boil them until the syrup is thick and clear.

QUINCE MARMALADE.

Rub the quinces with a cloth, cut in quarters ; stew them in a little water till tender enough to rub through a sieve. When strained, put a lb of brown sugar to a lb of flour ; set it on the fire, and cook slowly until enough to cut smooth.

ORANGE MARMALADE.

Boil the fruit, rub them through a sieve, take one pint of sugar to one of orange ; simmer slowly until it is a thick gell. Seal tight in jars.

BLANC MANGE.

Three pints sweet milk to half lb Irish moss; boil and stir frequently. sweeten to your taste, and flavor with vanilla or lemon. Strain through a bag, and turn into moulds.

MINUTE PUDDING.

One quart milk, two or three eggs, and a little salt. When tho milk boils, stir in flour until thick enough to cut with a spoon or knife. Sauce — cream and sugar ; flavor with nutmeg, lemon, and vanilla.

GINGER NUTS.

One cup sugar, one do. molasses, three eggs, half cup butter, half cup sour cream, one tablespoon ginger, half do. cloves, full teaspoon soda. Beat the sugar and eggs together till light ; melt the butter and molasses together ; add all together, with flour to make a soft dough ; roll, cut, and bake in a quick oven.

SPONGE PUDDING.

One lb sugar, twelve eggs, half lb flour, two tablespoons ground cinnamon. Beat the sugar and yelks together until very light, and the whites to a stiff froth ; add the flour with the white eggs, stirring very lightly. Sauce — half pint brandy, one pint water, two cups sugar, quarter lb butter ; flavor with peach. To be eaten while warm.

BAKED BERRY ROLLS.

Rub lard with flour with a little salt, water or milk to make sufficient dough ; roll thin ; spread over with berries; roll up the crust and put into a dripping-pan in rolls close together until full, then put into the pan butter, sugar and water ; bake slowly. Sauce — butter, sugar, brandy and water.

POTATO FERMENT ROLLS.

One pint of water, one do. sweet milk, one do. yeast, a little salt, flour enough to make a soft dough. When light, work in lard or butter if sour, work in a little soda with the flour, knead well, then break in a couple of eggs, knead well, make into small rolls, and set where it will keep warm ; it will rise in a few minutes ; bake in a quick oven.

APPLE JELLY.

Slice thirteen large apples very thin without paring them, then cover with water, boil and strain, and to the juice add a half lb white sugar, and as much lemon as your taste may direct. Clarify with egg, and boil to a jelly.

MUTTON CHOP PIC.

Stew the mutton and season. Paste the side of the dripping- pan, put in the meat with a strip of the crust rolled thin. Pour over it the gravy, and cover with a crust.

BAKED PEACH COBBLER.

Scald and rub the peaches ; stew until done ; season with sugar to your taste. Paste your pans, put in the fruit, dropping small pieces of butter over it ; cover with paste and bake. When done, float the pie with the syrup from the fruit.

COCOANUT PIE.

One large cocoanut grated, the milk of the same, and four rolled crackers. Boil two quarts of milk, a small piece of butter, four eggs, the rind of one grated lemon. Sweeten to taste ; paste at the bottom.

JUICE LEMON PIE.

Two lemons, three eggs, one teaspoon flour, little lump of butter, little salt; grate the rind of the lemon, squeeze out the juice, peel out the pulp; add all together; beat eggs, sugar, and lemon together; add sugar enough to fill a large bowl, and bake twenty minutes. This quantity will make two pies.

MACARONI.

One pound powdered sugar, one pound almonds, the whites of four eggs, two teaspoons extract lemon.

STEAM PLUM PUDDING.

One cup chopped beef suet, one cup molasses, one do. warm milk, one do. stoned raisins, one cup and a half flour, one teaspoon soda, cinnamon, cloves, and nutmeg, a little of each. Butter the dish, and steam four hours.

BISCUIT.

One quart milk, one tablespoon sugar, two do. butter, a little salt, three eggs, half cup yeast; have the milk as warm as the hand can bear. Stir quite stiff with flour.

LEMON PIE.

The grated rind and juice of one lemon, one cup powdered sugar, yolks of three eggs, two tablespoons flour, 3-4ths of a cup of water. Take the whites of the eggs and three tablespoons sugar, beat to a stiff froth, and turn it over the pie. When baked, set it in the oven again and brown it. Use but one crust.

CREAM PUFF.

Two cups flour, one do. butter, half pint water; boil the butter and water together; stir in the flour by degrees while boiling; cool it, then add five eggs and one-fourth of a teaspoon of soda. Drop on buttered tins, and bake in a quick oven. Dressing—One pint milk, one cup sugar, two eggs, half cup flour; beat the eggs, sugar, and flour together; stir them in the milk while boiling; flavor with vanilla. Break the cakes half round and fill with the cream, which should be made first. Do not beat the eggs for the cake or for the cream. This quantity makes about fifty.

MISS MADISON'S WHIM.

Two pounds flour, two do. sugar, one and a half do. butter, 12 eggs, one wine-glass brandy, two nutmegs and a half, one teaspoon soda, two pounds stoned raisins.

SWEET PICKLES.

Seven lbs tomatoes, four lbs sugar, one ounce cloves, two do. cinnamon, one quart vinegar. Pour the vinegar, with the spices and sugar, boiling hot over the fruit, three mornings in succession, then cook the fruit thoroughly; take it out, and boil the syrup as much as you like.

DELMONICO PUDDING.

One quart milk, three tablespoons corn starch; stir it in the milk just before boiling; boil three minutes; take yolks of five eggs and six tablespoons sugar; pour milk and starch on the eggs and sugar, flavor and salt. Pour it into the dish you wish to serve it in, and bake long enough to hold the icing. Beat the whites of the eggs with three tablespoons sugar, lay it over the pudding, set in the oven, and brown a little.

CREAM SPONGE.

Two eggs, one cup sugar; break the eggs in a cup, fill the cup with sweet cream, beat both together, one teaspoon soda, two do. cream tartar, rub cream tartar in the flour.

GINGER SNAPS.

Two cups sugar, two do. molasses, one cup and a half butter, one tablespoon ginger, one do. soda, one teaspoon cloves, two do. cinnamon, one cup sour milk, flour enough to make up.

BEEF SUET PUDDING.

Take suet, pick out all the strings and skin, then chop it very fine, mix with flour, season with pepper, salt, summer savory, sage, and sweet margery. Dress the inwards of the beef or of a pig as you would for sausage. Stuff them, and boil slowly nearly an hour, occasionally pricking them with a fork. When done, hang them up to dry; they are then ready for use at all seasons. Boil them over to warm when you wish to eat them.

CHICKEN SALAD.

Boil two or three chickens; when cold, slice off all the white meat, chop it fine, chop celery enough to season it well, mustard and black pepper to your taste; add strong vinegar, and the yolks of three eggs boiled hard and rubbed to a cream.

CHICKEN PIE.

Stew and season your chicken well. Bake a rich flaky pastry, lay it on a large platter, split the pastry in small pieces, laying between them the chicken and dressing.

INDIAN MEAL PUDDING.

Into one quart of boiling milk stir one quart sifted meal ; then add one quart cold milk, two well-beaten eggs, half teacup sugar, one do. flour, salt and spice to taste ; stir it well, and pour into a buttered dish ; bake two hours ; serve with butter.

STEAMED INDIAN PUDDING,

One pint sour milk, one do. sweet milk, one tablespoon sour cream ; stir in Indian meal to make a thick batter ; add one teaspoon soda, one do. salt ; steam three hours ; serve with sweetened cream. A handful of fruit, fresh or dried, stirred in, will be an addition.

CARROT PUDDING.

One lb flour, half lb potatoes, half lb suet, quarter lb sugar, half lb carrots ; chop the suet, carrots, and potatoes ; mix all well ; add raisins and currants ; boil three or four hours.

MRS. H.'S PUDDING.

One pint sweet milk, one teaspoon soda, half cup molasses, two cups Indian meal, one cup flour ; steam two hours.

BOILED PLUM PUDDING.

Take one lb suet chopped ; add one lb currants, one lb stoned raisins, one lb flour, one pint milk, eight eggs, and one nutmeg ; beat the eggs well ; mix thoroughly ; boil four or five hours.

POTATO PUDDING.

Two lbs potatoes boiled and mashed, half lb sugar, half lb butter, six eggs, one wine-glass brandy, and one nutmeg ; line a dish with paste, and bake.

EVE'S PUDDING.

Six ounces grated bread, six or seven chopped apples, six ounces sugar, six do. currants, six eggs, nutmeg to taste, six ounces suet chopped ; boil three hours.

KATE'S PUDDING.

One quart flour, two teaspoons cream tartar, one do. soda, one lb chopped suet, half lb currants, half lb raisins ; mix with cold water to a thick batter ; boil two hours ; eat with sauce.

KENTUCKY PUDDING.

One Cup and a half sugar, one cup butter, five eggs, one teaspoon soda, two do cream tartar, one cup milk, three do flour ; bake in a quick oven forty-five minutes.

COOKIES.

One cup butler, one do. sweet milk, two do. sugar, two teaspoons cream tartar, one do. soda, flour to roll ; roll thin, cut in small cakes; bake twenty minutes ; any seed you choose.

SUGAR SNAPS.

One cup butter, two do. sugar, three eggs, one teaspoon soda, one tablespoon ginger, flour to roll ; bake quick.

APPLE FLOAT.

Whites of two beaten eggs; add a spoonful of sugar, six apples stewed and drained until quite dry ; beat all together, then make a soft custard, put in the bottom of a dish, lay the float on top of it.

DRIED APPLE PUDDING.

Chop dried apples, wash and rub dry in flour; stir into a batter, and boil in a bag ; eat with butter sauce.

BLANC MANGE.

To two ounces of gelatine put three pints rich milk, flavor with lemon or vanilla, sweeten with white sugar. Put all on the fire cold, and stir frequently till all dissolve. Strain it, and when partially cool, pour into your moulds.

A-LA-MODE BEEF.

Take a round of beef, make a great many holes through it, roll strips of raw salt pork in a seasoning of one half teaspoon each of thyme, salt, pepper; and cloves. Draw through the holes these strips of pork. Put six onions, two tablespoons milk, and one quarter lb butter in a saucepan, stew them tender, put all into a pot, with, water enough to cover them; let it cook slowly five hours. Before taking up, add a pint of claret wine if you choose.

POTTED BEEF.

Take a beef shank, put it in water sufficient to cover it; boil till tender ; remove the bone and cartilage ; chop the meat fine, and put back into the kettle with the liquor, which should be one quart ; simmer gently ; season with salt, pepper, and mace to suit the taste. When cool, cut it in slices, to be passed around like dried beef. Potted beef can be kept any length of time by chopping fine, seasoning high, and packing hard in » stone jar, setting it in a cool place and covering closely.

PRESSED BEEF.

Sew tightly in a bag a round of beef, first sticking it full of cloves and pepper. When about half-done, throw into the water a handful of cloves, with salt, pepper, and mustard. When cold, take off the cloth, slice thin, and cat cold for tea.

BEST WAY TO ROAST BEEF.

Wash in warm water your beef, then rub in salt and pepper, and dry flour until a moisture rises on the meat; put it into a dripping-pan, setting it on a brick in the oven, keeping the bottom simmering, the top with a quick heat, turning the roast often till done. The juice that flows from the meat will cook it always sweet and tender.

FORCED STEAK.

Grind the steak through the mill, then put it out into rolls ; put into a saucepan one tablespoon lard, seasoning the steak with pepper and salt ; add a very little water. Simmer until done, turning often ; chop onions fine, laying over the meat ; baste the meat with the liquid and onions. When done, make a butter and cream gravy, and serve hot.

TURKEY POT PIC.

Cut the turkey into small pieces, and boil until done. Paste the dripping-pan with rich pastry, lay on the meat, cut small strips of dough, lay it among the meat, season with pepper and butter ; turn the gravy into the pan and cover with crust, cutting a place in the top, and bake moderately.

CALF HEAD SOUP.

Dress the head and boil until done, remove the bones from the meat, take all the meat from the upper part of the head and chop fine, and put it into the soup, with chopped potatoes and carrots, shives, pepper, salt, parsley, sweet margcry, and a little butter. Stir a little flour and milk together to thicken the soup. Make a hash of the meat from the under jaw. Take the brains from the head, beat up eggs as for an omelet, turn this over the brains after seasoning with salt and pepper. Melt some butter and turn on. Set it in the oven to cook slowly. Skin and slice the tongue ; put into a saucepan, with butter, pepper, and salt. Stew dry.

TO BOIL AND DRESS MUTTON HAM.

Perforate the ham, and put slices of onion in. Rub it with salt. Canvas the ham, put in whole grains of pepper and cloves ; sew it tight, and boil until done. Take three spoons sugar, one half pint Madeira wino, butter, thicken with flour ; boil and turn it over the ham with parsley.

TO COOK PARSNIPS.

Pare the parsnips and put them into a bag, season with salt, boil until done. When cold, slice, roll them in flour, and pepper them. Brown them in lard, and turn drawn butter over them.

TO COOK IRISH POTATOES.

Pare and boil quickly ; when done, turn into a colander. Mash them and dress with cream, butter, pepper and salt, pat them out into cakes and bake them. A good way is to put in the yelks of two or three eggs, and boiled codfish picked up fine, made into balls with the potato, buttered and baked.

HOW TO COOK AND DRESS OCHER.

Boil in clear water or with vegetables ; when tender, drain off the water ; dress it with butter, pepper and salt, and let it simmer or fry.

VEGETABLE OYSTERS.

Scrape and boil tender ; mash them, dress them with butter, salt and pepper. Pat them out and bake brown.

BEEF SOUP.

Take the shank bone, boil until tender; chop fine, potatoes, onions, and cabbage, and boil until done; season with salt, pepper, parsley, rosemary, or sweet margery. Rub the yelk of one egg into three tablespoons flour, rubbed into rolls and dropped into the soup to boil.

CHICKEN SOUP.

Boil one or two chickens whole with half a pint of rice until tender. Take out the chickens ; make a batter of sour milk, two or three eggs, a little soda, with flour ; drop this into the soup in spoonfuls; pepper and salt to taste. To dress the chickens, drawn butter and pepper. Boil three or four eggs hard and slice them, laying them over the chicken, with gell, sprigs of parsley.

HOW TO BOIL FISH.

Take pickerel, salmon, buffalo, or red horse ; rub them with a little saltpetre mixed with salt ; put inside the fish whole grains of pepper ; sew them up tight in a cloth and boil three hours. When done, turn them into a large platter ; dress with drawn butter and chopped parsley or rosemary.

FRICASEED CATFISH.

Boil in water with a little salt until done, then drain off the water, and turn over the fish rich cream, butter, pepper, and a little flour, and simmer slowly.

HAM OMELET.

Fry the ham about two minutes into a little hot fat, beat the eggs, season with salt and pepper ; mix a little flour and water into a batter, and stir into the eggs ; turn this over the ham, and turn quickly.

RICE OMELET.

Fat out into thin cakes cold boiled rice, beat the eggs and season, then drop the cakes into the egg, fry quickly, and turn into a platter and butter them.

FRIED OYSTERS.

Let the oysters stand in vinegar while you prepare a batter of eggs or milk and flour; season the batter to your taste; drop the oysters into the batter, and fry in butter or lard.

PICKLED ROAST PIG.

Dress and stuff your pig, put it into a dripping-pan and put it baking; take one pint of strong vinegar, Madeira wine, or currant wine, put into a basin with half lb butter ; boil together ; stir in a little batter made of flour and water ; baste the meat with this quite often until done.

MAGNETIC OIL.

One ounce chloroform, one do. laudanum, one do. tincture of colchicum, one do. capsicum, half do. castor oil, three do. alcohol.

BLACK OINTMENT.

One ounce red lead, one do. sweet oil, one do. linseed oil.

PELEG WHITE STICKING SALVE.

Seven pounds rosin, one pound beeswax, one pound mutton suet, two ounces gum arabic.

BARBERS' SHAMPOOING MIXTURE.

One pint soft water, one ounce sal soda, half ounce cream tartar. Applying a few spoonfuls, rub the roots of the hair thoroughly ; use a little warm water at the same time ; then wash well from the head and apply a little oil. This should be done once a week.

BARBERS' STAR HAIR OIL.

Castor oil six and a half pints, alcohol one pint and a half citronella and lavender oil half ounce each, mixed and well shaker.

COLOGNE.

Take oil rosemary and lemon each 1-4th oz., oil bcgamot and lavender each 1-8th oz., oil cinnamon eight drops, oils clove and rose fifteen drops, alcohol two quarts. Mix and shake well two or three times a day for a week.

TO CURE CORNS.

Soak the feet fifteen or twenty minutes, night and morning, in cool water ; remove at each time all which can be removed, without pain or bleeding; keep away all pressure.

Dentrifice, which removes tartarous adhesions, and induces a healthy action of the gums.

Dissolve oue ounce borax in one pint and a half boiling water ; when cool, add one teaspoonful tincture of myrrh and one tablespoonful of the spirits of camphor, and bottle for use. Take a tablespoonful of the mixture to the same amount of warm water, and apply at bed-time with a soft brush ; a stiff bristle brush should never be used, as they injure the gums.

BURNS.

After applying sweet oil. scrape the inside of a raw potato, lay it on the burn. In a short time put on fresh potato ; repeat it quite often ; it draws out the fire and gives immediate relief.

TOOTHACHE.

Alum reduced to powder two drachms, nitrous spirits of ether seven drachms ; mix and apply to the tooth ; this is a certain cure. Or put into the tooth a pill made of Camphor and opium.

RESTORING THE HAIR TO ITS ORIGINAL COLOR.

Lac Sulphuris two drachms, rose water eight ounces. Shake it thoroughly, and apply every night before going to bed.

CURE FOR RHEUMATISM.

One lb sarsaparilla, one do. prickly ash bark, one do. cherry bark off the root, one do. bittersweet root, half lb sweet fora, half lb wintergreen. Boil down to one gallon, and add one quart rum. Dose — one tablespoonful three times a day.

MAGIC OIL.

One ounce laudanum, one ounce chloroform, half ounce oil of sassafras, one ounce oil of hemlock, half ounce Cayenne pepper, one ounce oil cedar, half ounce camphor gum ; add two quarts aloohol.

ELIXIR PAREGORIC.

Opium three drachms, licorice hall 3-4ths ounce or six drachms, gum camphor three scruples or 1-8th ounce, oil anise two drachms or 1-4th ounce. Bruise opium and licorice line, put it into half pint boiling water, and steep until thoroughly dissolved ; put it into a bottle, add the oil anise, benzoin and camphor. Shake thoroughly several times in the course of twenty or thirty hours. It will then be fit for use.

CURE FOR CORNS.

Four ounces potash, two drops oil vitriol, one tablespoon alum pulverized.

CURE FOR DROPSY.

Queen of tne Meadow steeped in water without washing the roots.

GINGER POP BEER.

Five and a half gallons water, 3-4ths lb ginger root bruised, half ounce tartaric acid, two and 3-4ths lbs white sugar, whites of three eggs well beaten, one teaspoonful lemon oil, one gill yeast. Boil the root thirty minutes in one gallon of water. Strain off and put the oil in while hot. Make over night ; in the morning skim and bottle, keeping out the sediment.

ICE CREAM.

Half lb loaf sugar to a quart of cream or milk, boil a soft custard, six eggs to one quart of milk ; eggs to be beaten.

ANOTHER IS MADE AS FOLLOWS :

Boil one quart of milk ; stir into it, while boiling, one tablespoon arrow-root ; wet with cold milk ; when cool, stir in the yelk of an egg to give a rich color ; five minutes is enough to boil. In either receipt put in the sugar after they cool; keep the same proportions for any amount. The juice of strawberries or raspberries gives a color and flavor to ice creams — one ounce of extract to a gallon. Break the ice well, one quart salt to one pail ice. Half hour stirring and scraping down will freeze it.

TO PRESERVE MILK.

Put a spoonful of horse radish into a pan of milk, and it can be kept sweet for several days.

TO PRESERVE EGGS.

Eggs can be kept good for months by this preparation : one pint of coarse salt and one pint of unslacked lime in a pail of water. Keep cool.

www.ingramcontent.com/pod-product-compliance
Lightning Source LLC
Chambersburg PA
CBHW070107100426
42743CB00012B/2675